DON'T CLICK it!

No Strangers!

Sharrie Warner

Illustrations by Hinesman Dukes

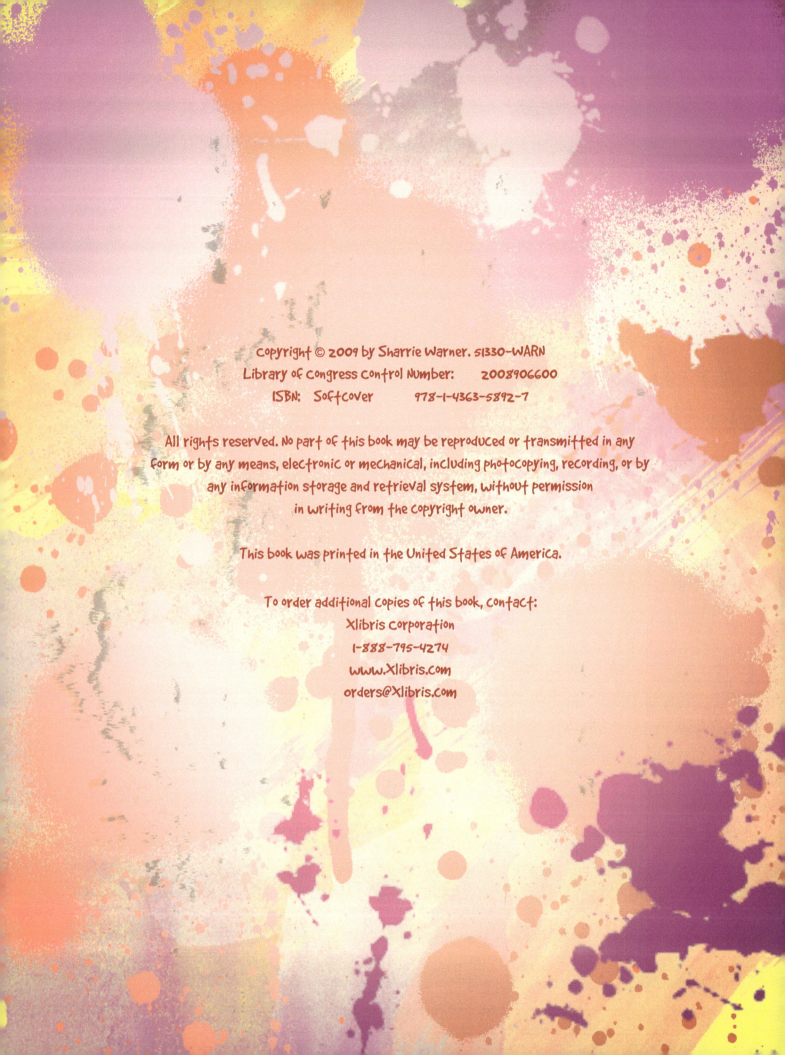

A Message from the Author

This book is about Internet safety.
Listen and learn.

Today in school, we talked about using the Internet and things to remember while using it.

Use good judgment when
using the Internet.

Get your parent's permission.

It only takes a second to log on to the wrong Web site.

Chat rooms can be dangerous!

Who are you chatting with?
Do you know?

Then don't Click it!

Remember to log off all Web sites!

17

CLICK
IT!

Parents should set a time limit!

Parents should monitor the Web sites their children surf daily.

If you use code words, vulgar language, and fictitious names, then that may not be the Web site for you.

Let's do the right thing!

25

BE SMART, BE SAFE,
AND DON'T CLICK IT!

27